# 360° LONDON

NICK WOOD

CARLTON BOOKS

The diagram shows degree markings: 0°/360°, 022.5°, 045°, 067.5°, 090°, 112.5°, 135°, 157.5°, 180°, 202.5°, 225°, 247.5°, 270°, 292.5°, 315°, 337.5°

## 360° LONDON IS ...

experiencing London shot in a complete circle, beyond the width of vision of the eyes. Imagine standing in a location, turning yourself through a complete circle and everything you see is shot in a series of overlapping images. The number of images depends on the focal length of the lens, but usually I shoot between 16 and 32 images.

The photographs in this book were shot with a Nikon digital camera mounted on a custom-made tripod, which kept the camera aligned accurately. The images were then "stitched" together using bespoke 360° software called Stitcher, made by AutoDesk.

For more information please see www.nickwoodphoto.com

# INTRODUCTION

## LONDON IS ...

**7.9 million** people speaking over **300** different languages

**8,452** miles of roads

**2,318** miles of bus routes and **181** miles of dedicated bus lanes

**270** miles of Underground and DLR train lines, covering **300** stations

**32** boroughs, **74** Parliamentary constituencies and **8** European constituencies

a **£140,190 million** annual economy – **18.5%** of the UK's GDP

a **£600 billion** daily turnover on the London Stock Exchange

**25.5 million** tourists per year – **57%** from overseas

## ... AND A GREAT PLACE TO SEE IN 360°

# I have travelled extensively for commissions to many parts of the world, but returning

**to London on the final approach to Heathrow Airport and seeing the snaking River Thames across the great metropolis evokes strong feelings for my home city. I have taken the River Thames, from east to west, as the theme and journey for this book and chosen to show the city in a series of 360° images.**

We experience life in 360°, so why not show it that way? The technology exists and this very honest form of photography has captured my imagination for more than 10 years.

Over many centuries London has been shaped by the very existence and geography of the River Thames. The deep tidal river was the artery to the centre of the UK for ships that brought cargo from the far corners of the world and left with goods and products bound for the Empire and beyond. The merchants grew in prosperity and London became one of the biggest ports in the world until containerization in the 1960s. The docklands of London sprawled over 65 square kilometres (25 square miles) to the east of the Pool of London, and today this same area is the location of a new trading centre – the gleaming steel and glass towers of the Canary Wharf Estate.

This global maritime hub attracted people from all over the world to live, work and trade. Today London is one of the most ethnically diverse cities in the world and so much the richer for it. London is home to approximately 7.9 million people speaking over 300 languages and practising more religions than any other city in the world. This diversity of population has shaped the fabric and atmosphere of one of the most iconic cites in the world.

The skylines and built environment are equally varied. The cutting-edge architecture of the towering Shard, Europe's tallest building, faces the medieval Tower of London across the Thames. The buildings have come to represent their place in history and London seems to have created an architectural icon to represent every era.

Over the years the world's most creative minds have been attracted to London – musicians, designers, chefs, artists and photographers have taken inspiration from the city and made London, one of the world's most creative environments, their home.

To me London is THE world city and through the images on the following pages I have attempted to bring to life why I enjoy being a very small part of this remarkable city.

**NICK WOOD**

# CONTENTS

▲ 090 **TRAFALGAR SQUARE**

▲ 092 **CABBIES' SHELTER**

▲ 094 **LONDON TAXI**

▲ 098 **ST PANCRAS INTERNATIONAL STATION**

▲ 100 **SOTHEBY'S AUCTION ROOM**

▲ 102 **PICCADILLY CIRCUS**

▲ 104 **PICCADILLY ARCADE**

▲ 106 **TRUMPER'S BARBERS**

▲ 108 **ST JAMES'S PARK**

▲ 110 **BUCKINGHAM PALACE**

▲ 112 **LIBERTY**

▲ 114 **CENTRAL LONDON PENTHOUSE**

▲ 116 **BAR ITALIA**

▲ 120 **SOHO DELI**

▲ 122 **CHINATOWN**

▲ 124 **HARRODS FOOD HALL**

**TOWER BRIDGE** ▶

**SOUTHWARK BRIDGE** ▲
**MILLENNIUM BRIDGE** ▶

**CHELSEA BRIDGE** ▶

◀ ALBERT BRIDGE

▲ BATTERSEA BRIDGE

◀ HAMMERSMITH BRIDGE

◀ RICHMOND BRIDGE

# THE THAMES IS …

The longest river in England

Measures **334** kilometres (**214** miles) from its source to the sea

Is **265** metres (870 feet) wide at London Bridge and **448** metres (1,470 feet) at Woolwich

Is home to over **55** sailing, rowing and canoeing clubs

Was given to the City of London in **1197** by Richard I for **1,500** marks

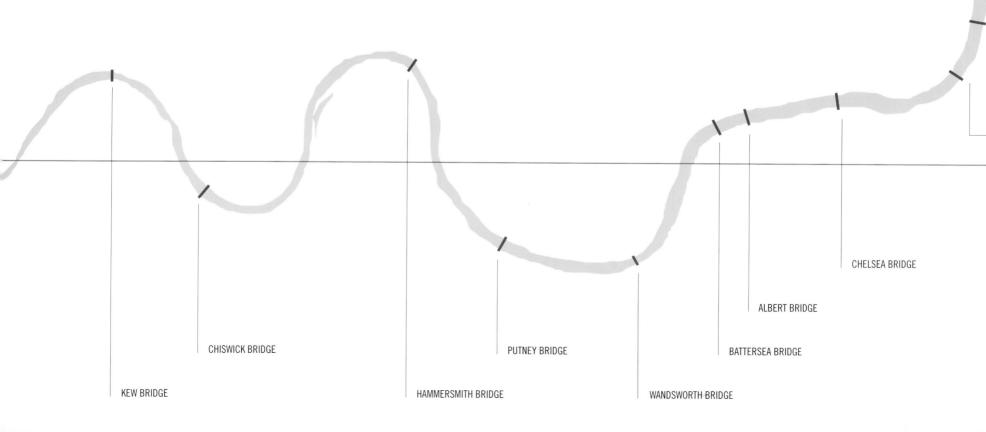

CHELSEA BRIDGE

ALBERT BRIDGE

BATTERSEA BRIDGE

PUTNEY BRIDGE

CHISWICK BRIDGE

WANDSWORTH BRIDGE

KEW BRIDGE

HAMMERSMITH BRIDGE

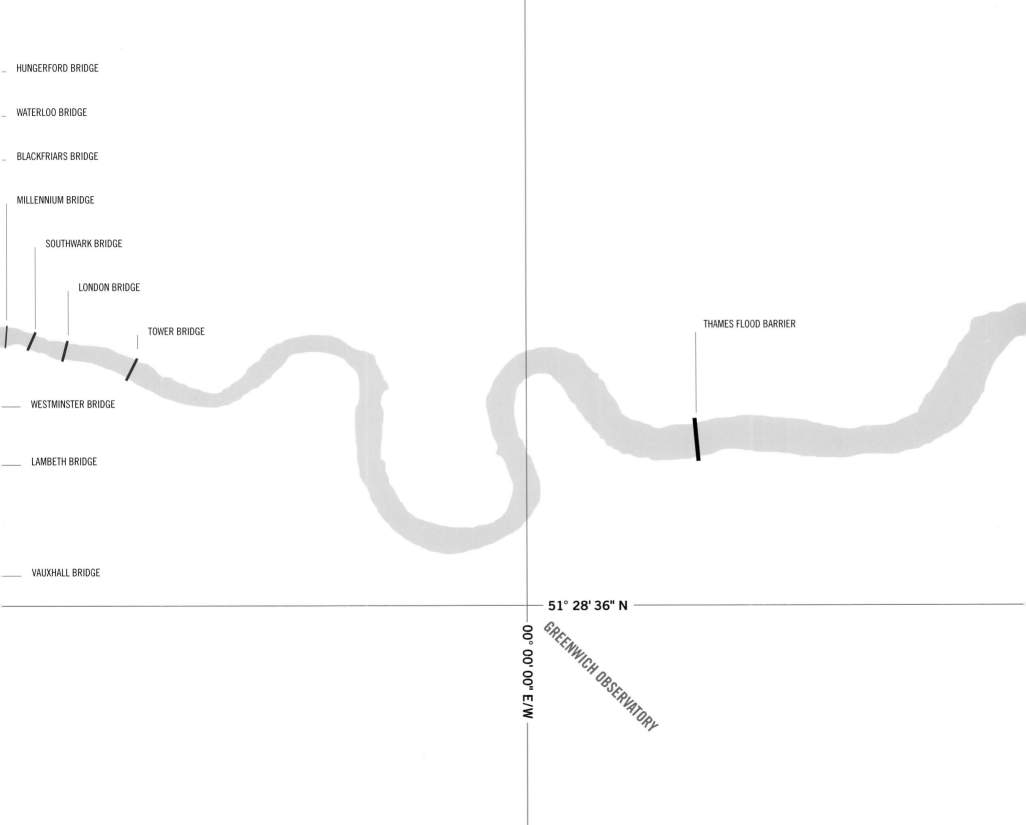

HUNGERFORD BRIDGE

WATERLOO BRIDGE

BLACKFRIARS BRIDGE

MILLENNIUM BRIDGE

SOUTHWARK BRIDGE

LONDON BRIDGE

TOWER BRIDGE

THAMES FLOOD BARRIER

WESTMINSTER BRIDGE

LAMBETH BRIDGE

VAUXHALL BRIDGE

51° 28' 36" N

00° 00' 00" E/W

GREENWICH OBSERVATORY

# THAMES FLOOD BARRIER EAST LONDON

AN ENGINEERING FIRST, THE BARRIER, completed in 1984, protects 324 square kilometres (125 square miles) of London from flooding. Tested monthly, it has been raised over 400 times due to exceptionally high tides. The 570-metre (1,870-foot) barrier consists of 10 3,175-tonne (3,500-ton) steel gates that can be raised in 30 minutes, and is expected to have a working life until around 2060. There are outline plans for a barrage across the Thames estuary between Southend in Essex and the north shore of Kent.

# GREENWICH OBSERVATORY GREENWICH

GREENWICH OBSERVATORY WAS DESIGNATED the centre of world time at the International Meridian Conference in Washington, DC in 1884. The dome surrounding its telescope was originally made of papier-mâché. It was destroyed by a flying bomb during World War II and replaced by a replica dome made from fibreglass. In 1894, the Observatory was subject to an anarchist bomb attack, an event immortalized in Joseph Conrad's novel *The Secret Agent*.

00° 00' 00"

## CUTTY SARK (overleaf)

THE FIGUREHEAD ON THE "LAST OF THE TEA CLIPPERS", the *Cutty Sark*, is Nannie, a wicked witch from the Robert Burns poem "Tam O'Shanter".

*Till first ae caper, syne anither,*

*Tam tint his reason a'thegither,*

*And roars out, "Weel done, Cutty-Sark!"*

*And in an instant all was dark.*

# THE O2 (PREVIOUSLY THE DOME) GREENWICH

BUILT ON RECLAIMED LAND TO HOUSE THE MILLENNIUM EXHIBITION and completed in 2000, the Dome was part of a project to regenerate the East End of London. The subject of huge controversy, it lay idle until 2007 when it became The O2, the world's most successful music venue, selling more than two million tickets annually. Designed by Richard Rogers, the 12 masts support the 52-metre-high (171-foot) tent made of PTFE fabric over 1 kilometre (0.6 miles) in diameter.

# CANARY WHARF DOCKLANDS

THE "NEW CITY OF LONDON" WAS BUILT IN 1987 in the East End Docklands, where many imports used to arrive from the Canary Islands. It covers 35 hectares (86 acres), and 95,000 people work there each day. The 244-metre-high (800-foot) One Canada Square has 4,388 steps and 3,960 windows. Lifts travel from the lobby to the 50th floor in just 40 seconds.

*One Canada Square contains 27,500 metric tonnes of British steel*

# JUBILEE LINE DOCKLANDS

IN 1999 THE JUBILEE LINE EXTENSION opened up Docklands to tube travellers for the first time. Each station was the work of a different architect: Canary Wharf station was designed by Foster and Partners (see page 146). Use of the line doubled when the extension opened, and over 185 million people now travel on the Jubilee Line each year.

# WHITECHAPEL BELL FOUNDRY EAST END

BRITAIN'S OLDEST MANUFACTURING COMPANY and the world's most famous bell foundry was established in 1570 during the reign of Queen Elizabeth I. They cast the original Liberty Bell (1752), the Great Bell of Montreal and, in 1858, Big Ben for the Palace of Westminster. Big Ben is the largest bell ever made at Whitechapel, weighing in at 13.7 tonnes (13½ tons), and a cross-section of the bell surrounds the foundry entrance door.

# LONDON'S AIR AMBULANCE EAST END

BASED ON A HELICOPTER PAD 40 metres (131 feet) above Commercial Road at the Royal London Hospital in the East End of the city, London's Air Ambulance (LAA) attends serious incidents within the confines of the M25, London's motorway ring road. The helicopter lifts within two minutes of an emergency call, with a senior trauma doctor and a specially trained paramedic on board. They can perform procedures normally only carried out in a hospital emergency department. Founded in 1989, the LAA has worked in some tricky places, including a pub, and once had to land in Piccadilly Circus. It has been involved in every major London incident and is funded by charitable donations.

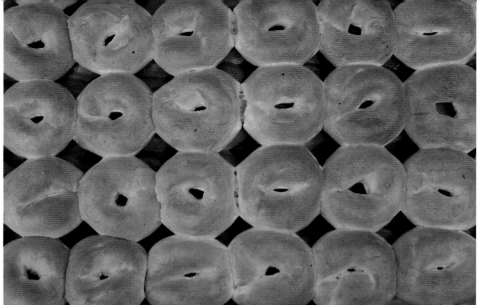

# BRICK LANE BAKERY EAST END

OPEN 24 HOURS A DAY, THIS FAMILY BUSINESS has been making 600 bagels per day since 1963, to an original recipe from Poland. An East End institution, it caters for everybody from city office workers to late night clubbers. To make eight bagels, you require: 475 grams (1 lb) strong plain flour, 220 millilitres (7⅔ fl oz) warm milk, 6 grams (⅛ oz) easy-blend yeast, 1 teaspoon of salt and 2 tablespoons of caster sugar.

# TOWER OF LONDON POOL OF LONDON

THE MOST PERFECT MEDIEVAL FORTRESS IN BRITAIN, the Tower was begun by William I in 1066. It has been the seat of British government, the home of kings and queens and a fearful prison. The Tower has housed leopards, lions and the famous ravens, as well as a polar bear – a gift from the King of Norway in 1252. The bear used to fish in the Thames while tethered by a chain.

*Anne Boleyn was beheaded on Tower Green in 1536*

# GREATER LONDON AUTHORITY POOL OF LONDON

DESIGNED BY FOSTER AND PARTNERS, this striking concrete and glass structure resembles an eyeball. The building leans back towards the south, where floor plates are stepped inwards from top to bottom, providing natural shading from the most intense direct sunlight. Water, extracted through two bore holes from the water table beneath London, is used to cool the building and for flushing the toilets.

# HMS BELFAST POOL OF LONDON

ABIGAIL WRIGHT IS THE ARTIST IN RESIDENCE ON HMS *BELFAST*, the former Royal Navy flagship now permanently moored in the Pool of London. She carves figureheads for shipping companies and private clients, and represents artists in the workspaces of London. HMS *Belfast* saw service in World War II and Korea before being opened to the public in 1971.

HMS Belfast was launched in 1938

# LLOYD'S BUILDING CITY OF LONDON

DESIGNED BY LORD ROGERS and built between 1979 and 1984, the headquarters of this unique insurance market is a fantastical, sci-fi construction. The working mechanics of the building – elevators, heating ducts, stairs, air conditioning – are on the outside of the structure, to free up interior floor space for the underwriters, who work on four floors covering a total of 10,590 square metres (113,990 square feet).

*Lloyd's no longer rings a bell for every loss at sea*

## CITY OF LONDON

The distinctive outline of the 180-metre (591-foot) Swiss Re building (centre right of skyline), which earned it the nickname "The Gherkin", has been a landmark on the City skyline since 2003, echoing the dome of St Paul's (centre left of skyline). Although dwarfing the nearby church of St Andrew Undershaft (far right), it is slightly shorter than Tower 42 (right), originally known as the NatWest Tower, which dates from 1979 and stands 183 metres (600 feet). From 2012 the number-one cloud-piercer in London will be the Shard (right of skyline), Europe's tallest building of the day at 310 metres (1,017 feet).

# LEADENHALL CITY OF LONDON

ESTABLISHED IN THE FOURTEENTH CENTURY around a manor house with a lead roof, the Leadenhall was London's best meat, game, fish and poultry market until it was destroyed in the Great Fire of London in 1666. Now it provides an oasis of calm for City workers escaping their desks at lunchtime. It's a far cry from the busy days of the eighteenth century, when a gander named Old Tom escaped slaughter at the poultry market and became a local celebrity. He died, aged 38, in 1835 and was buried in the market.

# BANK OF ENGLAND THREADNEEDLE STREET

*The Bank of England was set up in 1694 to finance the war against France*

## BANK OF ENGLAND

Founded in Cheapside in 1694, the Bank of England moved
to its current base in Threadneedle Street, at the hub of the
City, in 1734. The 1.2-hectare (3-acre) site includes three
floors of subterranean vaults where an unspecified fortune
in gold bullion is stored. Britannia, the seal of the bank, has
appeared on every bank note issued for over 300 years.

# SMITHFIELD MARKET HOLBORN

ALTHOUGH THREATENED BY PROGRESS and increased property prices, Smithfield has been London's premier meat market for 800 years, and approximately 142,410 tonnes (150,000 tons) of produce are traded in the market each year. A livestock market occupied the site as early as the tenth century; in 1173, William FitzStephen, a clerk to Thomas à Becket, described it as "a smoth field where every Friday there is a celebrated rendezvous of fine horses to be sold".

*Smithfield market pubs open at 6.30am*

CITY OF LONDON
WEST POULTRY
AVENUE EC1

CAUTION : BUSY MARKET AREA

THE CENTRAL COLD STORAGE

G.LAWRENCE
TODAY'S SPECIAL OFFERS
SiRLOiN SiRLOiN
STEAK £2.52 WHOLE
WHOLE £5.56kg £2.52 kg 5.56kg
OPEN TO THE PUBLIC 5AM – 2PM

CHICKEN GIZZARD £3.30 A BAG
CHICKEN WINGS £3.00 A BAG.

LAMB

LAMB

GRAND
AVENUE
EC1

DOMINE NOS
DIRIGE

CORPORATION
OF LONDON

Medusa

D&G
NICOLE FARHI
PRINGLE
LA PERLA
JOSEPH
SEE BY CHLOE
DKNY

COMMENCED
1867

# MILLENNIUM BRIDGE

A 325-METRE (1,066-FOOT) STEEL BRIDGE LINKING THE CITY OF LONDON at St Paul's Cathedral with the Tate Modern art gallery at Bankside, the Millennium Bridge is the first new pedestrian-only crossing over the Thames in more than a century. Designed by Foster and Partners and sculptor Sir Anthony Caro, the 4-metre-wide (13-foot) aluminium walkway is supported by cables which dip below the deck halfway across, allowing fantastic views of London.

# ST PAUL'S CATHEDRAL CITY OF LONDON

THE SITE OF A CHURCH SINCE AD 604, the Cathedral was designed and built by Sir Christopher Wren in 1697. Measuring 111 metres (365 feet) to the tip of the gold cross, the dome remains one of London's most iconic landmarks amongst the glass and steel of the new city. A climb up the 528 steps to the Golden Gallery is a must for any visitor. Many notable figures of British history have been laid to rest in the crypt. People of many religions have worshipped there over the years, including Martin Luther King, and a memorial service for Jordan's King Hussein included readings from the Koran.

# THE GLOBE THEATRE BANKSIDE

Bay E
→

BUILT IN 1598–99 BY CUTHBERT AND RICHARD BURBAGE, the original Globe Theatre numbered Shakespeare among its shareholders. After burning down in 1613, when a cannon fired during a performance of *Henry VIII* set the thatch alight, the theatre was rebuilt, only to be closed by the Puritans in 1642. The Globe was reconstructed and reopened to its original, in-the-round thatched design in 1993. Performers form a unique connection with the audience and, against their natural English reserve, groundlings standing near the stage are allowed to heckle.

# THE BLACK FRIAR PUB BLACKFRIARS

STANDING ON THE NORTH SIDE OF BLACKFRIARS BRIDGE, on the site of a former monastery, the glorious Black Friar is the only Art Nouveau pub in central London. It dates from 1875, and its ornate interior is decorated with jolly fat friars and pensive monks, moulded in marble and bronze, as well as quirky mottos and slogans. Some drinkers claim the Black Friar is haunted.

HASTE IS SLOW. WISDOM IS RARE

# THE BRITISH MUSEUM BLOOMSBURY

THE BRITISH MUSEUM IS A MUSEUM OF THE WORLD FOR THE WORLD. The collection houses more than seven million artefacts originating from every continent, illustrating the story of human culture from its beginnings. The reading room, originally designed by Sydney Smirke, was joined to the museum by a Foster and Partners' scheme featuring a 1,656-panel glass roof forming the largest covered square in Europe. Recent events at the museum include the virtual unwrapping of an Egyptian mummy to create a 3D journey through it, visualizing every feature and amulet, without any destructive and irreversible actual unwrapping.

# SOMERSET HOUSE THE STRAND

ORIGINALLY THE FIRST RENAISSANCE PALACE in England, today's building stands on the site of an earlier Tudor palace that was demolished in 1775. Until 1973 it was home to the General Register of Births, Deaths and Marriages; now it houses the Courtauld Institute art galleries. Every Christmas the central courtyard, which looks more like St Mark's Square, Venice than London, is transformed into a public skating rink.

**63**

# COVENT GARDEN WEST END

ORIGINALLY A SEVENTEENTH-CENTURY FLOWER AND FRUIT MARKET, and then dominated by brothels in the eighteenth century, Covent Garden has evolved into an unashamed tourist trap of souvenir stores, expensive eateries and strictly-timetabled street entertainers.

# LONDON CYCLE SCHEME

INITIATED BY MAYOR BORIS JOHNSON IN 2010, the bicycle hire scheme has created a cycling revolution in London. The scheme includes cycle "super highways" on main commuter routes, and is used by over a million Londoners. The fleet boasts 6,000 bicycles located in 400 docking stations, and hire is free for first 30 minutes. The bikes make an average of 20,000 journeys every day. Even royalty are fans, with reports that the Duke and Duchess of Cambridge have been keen users of the scheme.

# THE SOUTH BANK THE THAMES

COMPRISING THE NATIONAL THEATRE (above), the National Film Theatre, the Royal Festival Hall and the Hayward Gallery, the South Bank is a labyrinth of concrete halls and walkways and the centre of the arts in London. Critics are sharply divided on the aesthetic merits of this controversial monument to functionalism, but the centre, now a listed building, occupies a crucial place in London's cultural life.

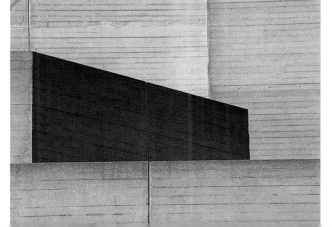

THE SOUTH BANK CENTRE HAS OVER 22 MILLION visitors each year. In summer its popular promenade along the River Thames throngs with street artists and performance groups of every imaginable genre.

# ARTIST'S STUDIO CLAPHAM

AT HIS SOUTH LONDON STUDIO, PAUL CATHERALL specializes in distinctive lino prints of the city's landmarks and architectural icons. Using a clean, sharp palette inspired by commercial art of the 1950s and 1960s, he has turned monuments such as Tate Modern, Battersea Power Station and the London Eye into affordable art.

# HUNGERFORD BRIDGE

ORIGINALLY A SUSPENSION BRIDGE designed by Brunel, Hungerford Bridge was modernized for the new millennium by architects Lifschutz Davidson. The two multi-span main footbridges are 320 metres (1,050 feet) long and 4.7 metres (15 feet) wide, and are suspended by arrays of cable stay rods from 25-metre-high (82-foot) inclined steel pylons. Unlike its predecessor, which ran alongside the train line into Charing Cross, it facilitates panoramic views of London.

# LONDON EYE SOUTH BANK

CONCEIVED AND DESIGNED BY HUSBAND-AND-WIFE TEAM David Marks and Julia Barfiield in 1993, the Eye took seven years and the skills of hundreds of people from five countries to build, and was opened during 2000 to celebrate the passing of the millennium. Privately funded, it immediately captured the public's imagination and it has become a modern icon of London. The 30-minute "flight" offers staggering views of the capital, and from the top it is possible to see around 40 kilometres (25 miles) across London and as far as Windsor Castle on a clear day. An average of 3.5 million visitors travel in the 32 capsules each year, reaching a height of 135 metres (443 feet) at the top, which is the equivalent to 64 red telephone boxes piled on top of each other.

# THAMES PANORAMA

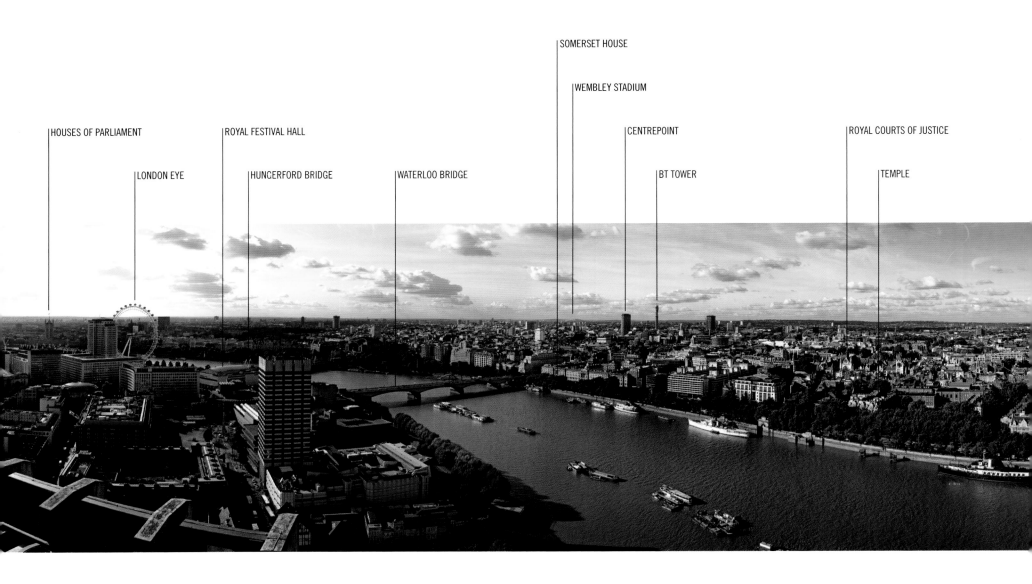

HOUSES OF PARLIAMENT

LONDON EYE

ROYAL FESTIVAL HALL

HUNGERFORD BRIDGE

WATERLOO BRIDGE

SOMERSET HOUSE

WEMBLEY STADIUM

CENTREPOINT

BT TOWER

ROYAL COURTS OF JUSTICE

TEMPLE

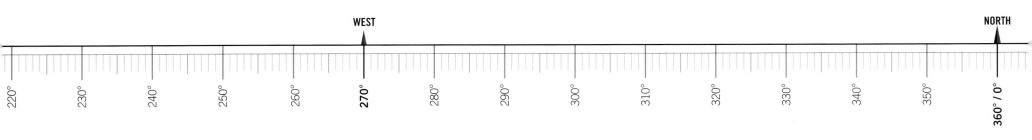

WEST

NORTH

220° 230° 240° 250° 260° 270° 280° 290° 300° 310° 320° 330° 340° 350° 360° / 0°

BLACKFRIARS BRIDGE

ST PAUL'S CATHEDRAL

TOWER 42

SWISS RE TOWER

MILLENNIUM BRIDGE

SOUTHWARK BRIDGE

TATE MODERN

TOWER OF LONDON

CANARY WHARF ESTATE

HMS *BELFAST*

TOWER BRIDGE

THE SHARD

GUY'S HOSPITAL

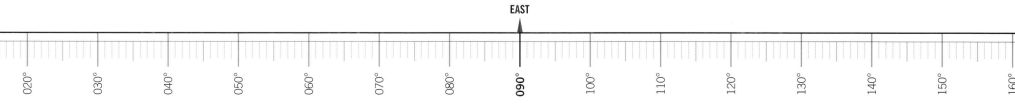

**EAST**

020°  030°  040°  050°  060°  070°  080°  **090°**  100°  110°  120°  130°  140°  150°  160°

# BIG BEN CLOCK TOWER WESTMINSTER

THE ARCHITECT SIR CHARLES BARRY SOUGHT HELP from the Queen's clockmaker Benjamin Lewis Vulliamy to design the magnificent clock tower in the same neo-Gothic style as the new Palace of Westminster. Together they designed the largest four-faced chiming clock in the world, each dial 7 metres (23 feet) in diameter, constructed from cast iron containing 312 pieces of opaque glass. The hour is struck by Big Ben itself, interim quarter-hours by the other bells. The Latin inscription carved in stone under each clock dial reads *"Domine Salvam fac Reginam nostrum Victoriam primam"*, which means "O Lord, save our Queen Victoria the First".

The clock tower of the Palace of Westminster is 96 metres high

# DUCK TOURS

THE NAME DUCK TOURS EVOLVED from the previous name for these peculiar amphibious craft: DUKWS. Ex-military vehicles, more than 21,000 were built to carry British troops for the D-Day landings in 1944. Now, five have been requisitioned to carry tourists past Parliament and through Trafalgar Square before taking to the Thames for the second half of the 70-minute tour of London.

# TRAFALGAR SQUARE WESTMINSTER

THE SPIRITUAL CENTRE OF LONDON, OVER THE YEARS the square has been the focus of celebration, protest, cultural events and festivals. It is home to St Martin-in-the-Fields church, the National Portrait Gallery and Nelson's Column, and is overlooked by four bronze lions designed by Sir Edwin Landseer in 1867. In 1876 the imperial measures of inches, feet, yards, links, chains, perches and poles were added to the north terrace wall and later relocated to outside the café when the central staircase was added. Three of the four plinths in the square are the bases for three sculptures, with the forth plinth home to changing art installations, such as Yinka Shonibare's scale model of Nelson's HMS *Victory* in a bottle.

# CABBIES' SHELTER VICTORIA

TAXI DRIVERS HAVING LUNCH AT AN OLD-FASHIONED CABBIES' SHELTER in Grosvenor Gardens near Victoria, central London. A Grade II listed building dating from 1870, this compact café and rest area is made of the sturdiest English oak. Solid, traditional meals are served up to working cabbies, with beef stew and dumplings, ham and eggs, and jam roly-poly all being house specialities.

93

# LONDON TAXI

TERRY, A TAXI DRIVER FOR 30 YEARS, arrives at the London Eye with passengers David Marks and Julia Barfield, the visionary husband-and-wife architect team who designed and created the Eye. The spectacular Eye, or Millennium Wheel, was raised to stand by the Thames in October 1999.

## THE FRENCH HACKNEY CARRIAGE

or "cab" (*cabriolet*) first appeared on London streets in 1820. Nowadays the spacious, familiar black taxi or cab is one of the capital's most familiar sights. There are more than 20,000 licensed taxis plying their trade in the capital, and every single driver has spent three to four years doing The Knowledge, the process of learning every one of London's complex streets and highways that is tested by a final exam.

# ST PANCRAS INTERNATIONAL STATION

THE CELEBRATED VICTORIAN STATION WITH ITS WILLIAM BARLOW-DESIGNED train shed narrowly escaped demolition in the 1980s. Connecting London to Europe, the high-speed Eurostar trains originate and terminate here. Eurostar operates up to 18 high-speed trains daily to Paris and nine to Brussels, and around nine million passengers use the service every year. The magnificent architecture of this grand station instills a great sense of arrival into a major world city.

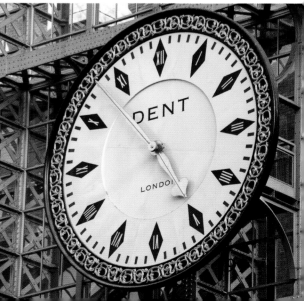

# SOTHEBY'S AUCTION ROOM

LONDON IS ONE OF THE MOST EMINENT ART CAPITALS IN THE WORLD, and it is fitting that it is home to Sotheby's. Both contemporary and classic art auctions take place in 10 salerooms worldwide and Sotheby's conducts 250 auctions every year in over 70 categories. The first international auction house to expand from London to New York, Sotheby's is the oldest publicly traded company on the New York Stock Exchange. Modern technology allows bidders to place bids in real time from anywhere in the world, and Sotheby's holds numerous world records, including the highest price for any Old Master Painting sold at auction, being $76.5 million.

# PICCADILLY CIRCUS WEST END

*Piccadilly gets its name from a seventeenth-century inhabitant,*

FAMOUS FOR ITS BRIGHT LIGHTS, and a tourist Mecca, Piccadilly Circus contains a famous bronze statue of a winged archer atop a fountain. The figure is called Eros, the god of love, but was designed in the nineteenth century as a monument to Lord Shaftesbury, a noted philanthropist. To the right of the neon signs, Shaftesbury Avenue leads into theatreland.

*a dressmaker who specialized in a frilly collar called a picadil*

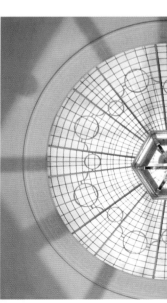

# PICCADILLY ARCADE WEST END

BUILT IN 1910 IN GEORGIAN STYLE, the meticulous bow-fronted shops of this upmarket arcade are light years away from the bawdy bustle of Piccadilly and Oxford Street. Specializing in bespoke tailors, china, jewellery and luxury goods, this is retail therapy for aristocrats: the nouveau riche need not apply. Benson & Clegg, suppliers of buttons and badges to the Prince of Wales, have occupied their site since 1937.

# TRUMPER'S BARBERS MAYFAIR

THIS STATELY OLDE WORLDE BARBER SHOP has scarcely changed since Mr George Trumper established Geo F Trumper, Perfumers and Barbers, in Mayfair's Curzon Street in 1875. The establishment has trimmed the beards and waxed the eyebrows of "London gentlemen and members of the Royal Court" for over 135 years, earning the Royal Warrant from Queen Victoria and five subsequent monarchs.

# ST JAMES'S PARK WESTMINSTER

EVERYBODY LOVES LONDON'S GREEN AND SPACIOUS PARKLANDS, and St James's Park, the oldest of the capital's royal parks, consists of 36 hectares (90 acres) of beauteous splendour. Joggers, families and workers enjoying a lunchtime sandwich gather in this public space between The Mall to the north and Birdcage Walk to the south. Pelicans, a gift from a seventeenth-century Russian ambassador, are fed every day at 3pm near Duck Island Cottage.

*St James's Park took its name from a hospital for leper women*

# BUCKINGHAM PALACE WESTMINSTER

TOURISTS FLOCK DAILY TO THE LONDON HOME OF THE BRITISH ROYAL FAMILY, but its inhabitants have not all been keen on the imposing dwelling. "The vast building with its endless corridors and passages seemed pervaded by a curious, musty smell," wrote King George V. "I was never happy there." The Royal Family occupy few of the 600 rooms in the Palace: the Queen and Duke of Edinburgh have a suite of about 12 rooms on the first floor, overlooking Green Park. Each summer the Queen holds three garden parties here, inviting around 8,000 guests.

# LIBERTY WEST END

ARTHUR LASENBY LIBERTY FOUNDED LIBERTY IN REGENT STREET, one of London's most prestigious department stores, in 1874. It specialized in selling *objets d'art*, fabrics and ornaments from the Orient. In 1924 the store's Tudor shop was built from the timber of two ships, HMS *Impregnable* and HMS *Hindustan*. The famous rug department, with the air of a Turkish bazaar, occupies a floor of this building.

# CENTRAL LONDON PENTHOUSE MAYFAIR

THIS FIFTH-FLOOR PENTHOUSE in Mayfair is the very essence of swanky central London living. Owned by a young entrepreneur businessman and his wife, this fabulous south-facing property, built in 1910, is within walking distance of Green Park, Trafalgar Square and Buckingham Palace.

# BAR ITALIA SOHO

A MAGNET FOR FASHION VICTIMS, early-hours revellers and aficionados of the perfect cappuccino, Frith Street's 24-hour Bar Italia is a place to people-watch and be seen. It's also the base for the Bar Italia Scooter Club, whose members congregate on their Vespas and Lambrettas most Sunday evenings. Around the corner from the sex and sleaze of Soho, this is a very innocent pleasure.

CLASSIC
MUSICALS

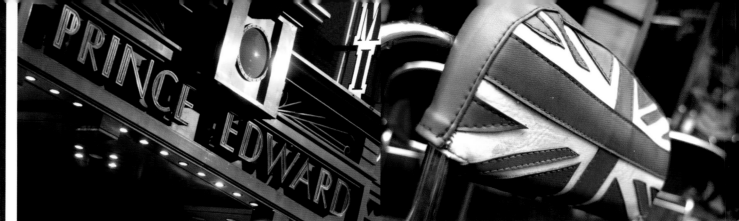

PRINCE
EDWARD

Les
Misérables

LONDON COUNTY COUNCIL
IN 1926
IN THIS HOUSE
JOHN LOGIE
BAIRD
1888-1946
FIRST DEMONSTRATED
TELEVISION

"WHAT
BRILLIANT
JOKES
THROUGHO...

NORMAN'S

THE
WEST END'S
BEST
KNOWN
PUB

Traditional
BEERS & LAGER

# SOHO DELI WEST END

ONE OF THE MANY HIDDEN PLEASURES OF SOHO is its numerous delicatessens run by the Italian community, which stock every kind of foodstuff imaginable, and quite a few more besides. Simply duck through the door of one of these capacious Aladdin's caves and lose yourself in sensory overload.

# CHINATOWN SOHO

LONDON IS AN EVER-SHIFTING MOSAIC of myriad ethnic groups, and has hosted a vibrant Chinese community since the late nineteenth century. The largest influx arrived at the end of the 1950s, when many enterprising London Chinese bought or leased property in a then scruffy Soho thoroughfare called Gerrard Street and opened restaurants. Unsurprisingly becoming known as Chinatown, the area was later pedestrianized and large, ornate Chinese gates and street furniture were installed.

*London's first Chinese restaurant opened in 1908*

# HARRODS FOOD HALL KNIGHTSBRIDGE

THE WORLD-FAMOUS HARRODS began as a small grocer shop in Knightsbridge in 1849, and food remains a major priority for the original aristocrat's department store. During World War II, the store employed a cookery expert to advise customers how best to use their wartime rations. To the left of the palatial fish hall on the lower ground floor, well-heeled customers can slide onto a high stool and lunch on oysters.

# NATURAL HISTORY MUSEUM SOUTH KENSINGTON

LOCATED IN SMART SOUTH KENSINGTON, the Natural History Museum is a centre of excellence in taxonomy and biodiversity. Founded in 1811, its 1.2 hectares (3 acres) of gallery space can display only a tiny percentage of the museum's whole collection. Visitors to the Life Gallery, below, are immediately confronted by a 26-metre (85-foot) skeleton of a Diplodocus dinosaur.

# LEIGHTON HOUSE MUSEUM HOLLAND PARK

HIDDEN IN THE LEAFY RESIDENTIAL STREETS OF HOLLAND PARK in West London, Leighton House is a gem of a museum. The opulent home and studio was created and built in 1865 by the Victorian artist Frederic Lord Leighton and is a monument to Moorish architecture. The Arab Hall that forms the centrepiece is decorated with over 1,000 Islamic tiles, mostly from Syria.

# SOLAR SHUTTLE HYDE PARK

THIS SOLAR-POWERED BOAT GLIDES BETWEEN the Diana, Princess Of Wales Memorial Fountain on the south side of the Serpentine and the boat house on the northern edge of the lake using the rays of the sun to power its two silent electric motors. The 27 curved panels that form the roof produce 2kW of energy. It can reach a speed of 8 kph (5 mph) and produces no emissions.

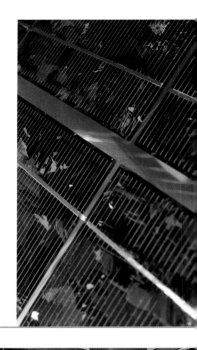

# THE ALBERT MEMORIAL KENSINGTON

SITUATED ON THE SOUTHERLY EDGE OF HYDE PARK, the glistening, spruced-up statue of Queen Victoria's beloved husband, with its Gothic-style sculpted canopy, has not always been so shiny. Originally completed in 1875, for 80 years it was covered in black paint, although it is not certain whether this was as camouflage against German attacks during the First World War or as defence against pollution in preceding years. It was restored in the 1990s and again in 2006. The hall that bears his name is highly popular concert venue nearby, known for its annual Prom concerts.

**133**

# ELGIN CRESCENT NOTTING HILL

LOCATED AT THE HEART OF WEST LONDON'S achingly trendy Notting Hill district, the elegant town houses of Elgin Crescent offer a very English take on comfortable living. Beautifully kept and immaculately tended, these pricy, bijou residences are a short stroll away from the hip restaurants and world-famous antiques market at Portobello Road.

# NARROW BOAT LITTLE VENICE

MIKE SITS IN THE BOATMAN'S CABIN aboard his boat *Beauideal*, moored at Little Venice, a leafy suburb of north-west London. In the working days of such boats, families would live in this tiny space, sleeping on beds that folded down from the wall, while the rest of the craft was given over to the cargos of the Industrial Revolution such as coal, wool and timber. *Beauideal* is 14 metres (46 feet) long and 2 metres (7 feet) wide, and Mike travels the waterways for pleasure.

*London has 145 kilometres of canals*

# NEASDEN TEMPLE BRENT

THE LARGEST HINDU TEMPLE OUTSIDE INDIA, Neasden Temple was constructed from 4,540 tonnes (5,000 tons) of Italian marble which were sent to India where they were carved in the traditional style then shipped to London. Unusually, no steel was used in its construction. The deities, whose colourful clothing is changed daily, and the silence found among the Pillars of Divinity are conducive to prayer and meditation. The temple also contains a museum of Hinduism and a visitor centre that attracts more than 500,000 visitors per year.

Pragat Brahmaswarup Pramukh Swami Maharaj
प्रगट ब्रह्मस्वरूप प्रमुख स्वामी महाराज

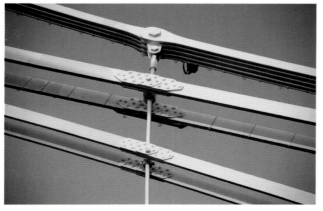

# ALBERT BRIDGE THE THAMES

LINKING CHELSEA ON THE NORTH SIDE of the Thames with Battersea on the south, the gracious Albert Bridge is an elegant iron suspension bridge, which later had pillars placed under its centre when heavy traffic began to threaten its structure. On the north side of the bridge stands a nowadays rare original red telephone box and a rather quixotic notice ordering soldiers to break step when they cross the Albert.

# BATTERSEA DOGS HOME BATTERSEA

THE ENGLISH ARE RENOWNED ACROSS THE WORLD for their love of dogs. Now over 150 years old, Battersea Dogs Home is a uniquely English institution. Every stray dog picked up by the Metropolitan Police is brought to Battersea, where loving staff look after, retrain and, hopefully, rehome them. On any given day there are between 300 and 600 lost, stray or unwanted dogs at Battersea.

*Every Battersea dog is walked five times per day*

DEDICATED
IN LOVING MEMORY
OF OUR BEAUTIFUL
LITTLE
LUCY II

# FOSTER'S STUDIO BATTERSEA

FOSTER AND PARTNERS ARCHITECTS. LORD FOSTER and his colleagues are involved in shaping unique buildings and reinventing London for the twenty-first century. Even in these days of virtual space and digital design, they still use their model shop to produce 3D models to convince often sceptical planners and the public of the merits of their architectural creations. Trafalgar Square is to the left, the Greater London Authority building on the central table.

_ Foster's model shop "plants" about 17,000 scale trees every year

# LONDON BUSES STOCKWELL

BUS DRIVER LIONEL GAVE UP HIS JOB TO ACHIEVE HIS AMBITION of driving a Routemaster bus on the roads of London. The traditional Routemaster buses, with their unique open backs, were officially phased out in 2005, on safety grounds. But a new design was commissioned and a prototype was due to take to the streets of London in 2011.

# BRIXTON MARKET BRIXTON

SINCE THE 1950S BRIXTON has been dominated by London's West Indian population. In its bustling covered market, salt fish ackee, beef jerky and yams fight for space with incense sticks and cheap 'n' cheerful Bob Marley T-shirts, as reggae and hip-hop boom out of ghetto-blasters. It's had its social problems, but Brixton remains a community like no other in London.

*Former British Prime Minister John Major grew up in Brixton*

# CRYSTAL PALACE DINOSAURS CRYSTAL PALACE

HIDDEN AMONG THE TREES AND BUSHES OF CRYSTAL PALACE PARK are the world's first life-sized dinosaur sculptures. Created by Benjamin Hawkins and palaeontologist Richard Owen in the 1850s, these lifelike monsters created quite a stir and started the modern obsession with dinosaurs – small models were even created for a fascinated public. The not-strictly-anatomically-correct monsters are now Grade I listed monuments (along with Buckingham Palace and the Royal Albert Hall!).

# THE TUBE CLAPHAM COMMON

LONDON UNDERGROUND OPERATES 400 KILOMETRES (250 MILES) OF RAILWAY LINE, of which less than 50 per cent is actually underground. The highest point is at Amersham on the Metropolitan Line, 152 metres (500 feet) above sea level; the deepest station is Hampstead, 59 metres (194 feet) below ground level. The busiest line is the District Line, which carries 180 million passengers per year.

# KEW GARDENS RICHMOND

THE ROYAL BOTANIC GARDENS AT KEW cover an area of just over 120 hectares (300 acres) and house the largest and most comprehensive living plant collection in the world. The Grade I listed Palm House, built between 1844 and 1848, resembles a lush indoor Brazilian rain forest. The conceptual genius of architect Decimus Barton was to make the curved glass panes, of which there are 16,000, mimic the shape of giant tropical leaves and foliage.

THIS IS A CARLTON BOOK

This edition published in 2012 by Carlton Books
An imprint of the Carlton Publishing Group,
20 Mortimer Street
London
W1T 3JW

Photographs © Nick Wood 2003, 2012
Text and design © Carlton Books Limited 2003, 2012

Photography conceived and shot by Nick Wood

A CIP catalogue record for this book is available from the British Library.

ISBN: 978 1 84732 603 4

Printed in China

**DESIGNER** Ceri Hurst

**CAPTION WRITER** Ian Gittins

**EDITORS** Sarah Larter and Stella Caldwell

**PRODUCTION** Lucy Woodhead

# ACKNOWLEDGEMENTS

During the photography and production of a complex book such as this there are many people who contribute their skills and expertise in many different ways at various stages of its creation.

**THANK YOU**... to my assistants Clare Miller and Graham Carlow who helped not just during the photography, but also during the post-production process.

**THANK YOU**... to Clare Baggaley and her team at Carlton books; Vanessa Daubney; Ceri Hurst; Lucy Coley and Maria Petalidou.

**THANK YOU**... to Rosie Richer, Abigail Cooke, Andrew Aldwinkle, Paul Catterall, Terry the taxi, Chris Jenner and the cabbies in the Grosvenor Square shelter, Peter Scott at the Serpentine boathouse, David Marks and Julia Barfield, Al and the Bar Italia scooter club, Mike Dedman, Louise King, Diane Middleton, Steve Riddell, Tim Harris and the helicopter team at The Whitechapel Hospital, Alexandra Burla and her birds, Peter Scott at the Serpentine Boathouse, Sandra Roatz at Strata, Kate Hoey, Hayes Davidson, Hannah Talbot, Vanessa Minet, Rachel Preece, Lydia Shallett, Lynda Doggett, Claire Brown, Yogesh Patel and Shaumit Saglani at Neasden Temple.

**AND LAST BUT BY NO MEANS LEAST**, thank you to the many Londoners who helped in may ways, enabled access to rooftops, allowed me into private spaces, and to those who contributed their time, enthusiasm and interest during the photography of this book.

## NICK WOOD 2012

www.nickwoodphoto.com

www.londonpanoramic.co.uk

FOR FURTHER INFORMATION ABOUT SOME OF THE PEOPLE AND COMPANIES WHO WERE INVOLVED WITH THIS PROJECT:

www.whitechapelbellfoundry.com

www.bankofengland.co.uk

www.theartsmovement.com

www.london.gov

www.shakespears.globe.org

www.tate.org

www.southbanklondon.com

www.liberty.co.uk

www.ducktours.com

www.harrods.com

www.thetube.com

www.kew.org

www.fosterandpartners.com

www.dogshome.org

www.somerset-house.org.uk

www.marksbarfield.com

www.hayesdavidson.com

www.trumpers.com

www.nhm.ac.uk

www.paulcatterell.com

www.landonsairambulance.co.uk

www.royalparks.gov.uk

www.solarshuttle.co.uk